Mindful Eating, Mindful living

Cultivating Balance and Fulfillment

Dr. Jeffrey R Crawford

Copyright © Dr. Jeffrey R.Crawford(2024)

All rights reserved. No part of this publication may be reproduced, distributed, or transmitted in any form or by any means, including photocopying, recording, or other electronic or mechanical methods, without the prior written permission of the publisher, except in the case of brief quotations embodied in critical reviews and certain other noncommercial uses permitted by copyright law. For permission requests, write to the publisher at the address below.

Declaimer

This book is intended for informational purposes only and is not intended as financial, investment, legal, or tax advice. The author and publisher disclaim any liability or responsibility for any loss or damage incurred as a result of the use of the information presented in this book. Readers are advised to consult with a qualified professional before making any financial, investment, legal, or tax decisions.

While every effort has been made to ensure the accuracy and completeness of the information presented in this book, the author and publisher make no representations or warranties of any kind, express or implied, about the completeness, accuracy, reliability, suitability, or availability with respect to the information, products, services, or related graphics contained in this book for any purpose. Any reliance you place on such information is therefore strictly at your own risk

Table of content

Introduction

Chapter 1:
The Foundations of Mindful Eating
    Principles of Mindful Eating
    The Science Behind Mindful Eating
    Mindful Eating in Everyday Life
    The Transformative Power of Mindful

Chapter 2:
Developing Awareness in Eating Habits
    Identifying Hunger and Fullness Cues
    Emotions and Dating
    Mindful Eating Exercises
    Quotes About Mindful Dating

Chapter 3:
Mindful Living
Understanding Emotional Balance.
    The Importance of Mindfulness in Emotional Balance
    Effective Mindfulness
    Bringing Mindfulness into Everyday Life

Overcoming Challenges in Mindful Living
Inspirational Quotes About Mindful Living
Developing a Mindful

Chapter 4:
Recognising and Managing Mood and Anxiety
Understanding Mood Disorders
Understanding Anxiety Disorders
The Role of Mindfulness in Managing Mood and Anxiety
Effective Mindfulness
Addressing Specific Triggers and Situations.
The Effect of Lifestyle on Emotional Balance
Quotes to Inspire and Guide
Developing a Personal Mindfulness

Chapter 5:
Create a Mindful Eating Plan
Principles of Mindful Eating
Steps to Create a Mindful Eating Plan
Plan Balanced Meals
Developing a Structured Eating Schedule
Setting Up Mindful Eating Spaces
Practice Mindful Eating Techniques
Reflecting and Adjusting Your Plan
Inspirational Quotes About Mindful Eating

Chapter 6:
Nurturing the Body and Mind with Intention

The concept of nourishment
The Relationship Between Food and Mood
Mindful Eating Physical Health
Strategies for Intentional Nourishment
Meal Planning With Intention
Mindful Grocery Shopping
Cooking and eating mindfully
The role of hydration
Emotional and Social Aspects of Eating
Quotes to Encourage Mindful Nourishment

Chapter 7:
Strategies to Overcome Emotional Eating
- Understanding Emotional Eating.
- Recognising the Signs of Emotional Eating.
- Strategies for Overcoming Emotional
- Developing Self-Awareness
- Practice Mindfulness
- Identifying Alternative Coping Strategies
- Healthy coping strategies:
- Seeking Professional Support
- Inspirational Quotes About Emotional Eating

Chapter 8:
Bringing Mindfulness into Daily Life
- Understanding Mindfulness.
- Benefits of Mindfulness
- Practical Approaches to Integrating Mindfulness into Daily Life

Developing Mindful Habits
Inspirational Quotes about Mindfulness

Chapter 9:
Dealing with Food Cravings and Temptation
    Understanding Food Cravings.
    Strategies for Managing Food Cravings:
    Mindful Eating for Craving Control
    Dealing with Temptations
    Quotes that Inspire Resilience

Chapter 10:
Promoting Mindful Living for Long-Term Wellness
    The Importance Of Mindful Living
    Effective Strategies for Long-Term Wellness

Chapter 11:
Strategies for Sustainable Habits and Lifestyle Changes.
    The Importance of Sustainability
    Strategies for Sustainable Habits Building
    Overcoming Common Challenges
    Developing Healthy Habits for Life
    Quotes to Inspire Sustainable

Conclusion:

Introduction

In today's fast-paced society, many of us rush through meals, eat on the go, and hardly taste or savor our food. This quick, mindless eating habit can have serious effects for our physical health, mental well-being, and general quality of life. My personal experience with mindful eating began a few years ago, when I realized how disconnected I had become from the simple act of eating. Meals were no longer a source of nourishment and delight, but rather a rushed necessity crammed into an already jam-packed schedule.

One evening, after a particularly stressful day, I found myself mindlessly devouring an entire bag of chips while watching television. When I reached for another chip and saw the bag was empty, it hit me: I couldn't even remember the taste of what I had just eaten. This moment of realization triggered a significant shift in my life. I set out on a journey to understand and practice mindful eating, which revolutionized not only my relationship with food but also my overall approach to life.

This book is the climax of that trip. It is intended to guide you towards a more mindful way of eating and living, allowing you to reconnect with your body, mind, and soul. The fundamentals of mindful eating are simple but effective. By focusing on the present moment and being completely aware of our eating experiences, we can break away from bad patterns and discover more satisfaction and joy in our meals.

Mindful eating is more than just eating; it is about developing a deeper understanding of how we live. It helps us to slow down, enjoy the present moment, and make decisions that benefit our overall health. This practice can have a significant impact on our physical health, such as improved digestion and weight management, as well as our mental health, by reducing stress and increasing relaxation.

By purchasing this book, you are taking a significant step towards a better, more conscious lifestyle. Whether you are young or elderly, new to mindfulness or trying to develop your practice, this book provides essential insights and strategies for changing your relationship with food and improving your general well-being. Accept this trip with an open heart and mind, and learn the amazing impact that mindful eating and living can have on your life. Welcome to a new way of eating and living, where every mouthful and moment is an opportunity for mindfulness and delight.

Chapter 1:

The Foundations of Mindful Eating

Mindful eating is a technique founded on the ancient concepts of mindfulness, which is giving whole attention to the current moment without judgment. When it comes to eating, mindfulness helps us to be completely present in the sensory experience tasting, smelling, and savoring each bite as well as the physical sensations of hunger and satiety.

At its foundation, mindful eating is about developing a better understanding of our relationship with food. It encourages us to slow down, enjoy the act of eating, and make informed decisions that benefit our health and well-being. Unlike dieting, which frequently entails harsh rules and limits, mindful eating is a flexible, nonjudgmental strategy that promotes a healthy relationship with food.

Benefits of Mindful Eating

The advantages of mindful eating extend well beyond the dining table. Mindful eating can help us enhance our physical health, mental well-being, and general quality of life.

Here are several significant advantages:

1. Improved Digestion: Eating slowly and completely promotes digestion, helping the body to absorb nutrients more efficiently.

2. Weight control: Mindful eating, which pays attention to hunger and fullness cues, can help prevent overeating and promote healthy weight control.

3. Enhanced Food Enjoyment: Mindful eating encourages us to savor each bite, which increases our contentment and enjoyment of our meals.

4. Reduced Stress: Mindfulness activities, such as mindful eating, have been demonstrated to lower stress and improve relaxation.

5. Better Emotional Health: Mindful eating can help us identify and resolve emotional eating behaviors, resulting in a healthier relationship with food.

Principles of Mindful Eating

Understanding and practicing mindful eating requires familiarity with its key ideas.

Here are some fundamental concepts:

1. Awareness: Mindful eating entails focusing on the present moment, observing the flavors, textures, and scents of food, as well as our physical experiences and emotions.

2. Non-judgment: Practicing non-judgment entails accepting our eating experiences without criticism or guilt. It entails examining our routines and behaviors with interest and compassion.

3. Savoring: Savoring is really experiencing and savoring our food. It entails slowing down and savoring the sensory aspects of each bite.

4. Listening to Our Bodies: Mindful eating urges us to pay attention to our bodies' hunger and fullness cues, eating only when we are hungry and stopping when we are satisfied.

5. **Cultivating appreciation:** Practicing appreciation entails appreciating the food we eat while also acknowledging the effort and resources put into getting it to our table.

The Science Behind Mindful Eating

Mindful eating has been linked to improved physical and emotional wellbeing, according to research. According to studies, mindful eating can enhance digestion, blood sugar regulation, and minimize symptoms of gastrointestinal illnesses.

Furthermore, mindful eating has been linked to healthy eating habits, such as greater consumption of fruits and vegetables and lower consumption of processed foods.

One study published in the journal *Appetite* discovered that participants who exercised mindful eating reported more enjoyment of meals and were less prone to overeat than those who did not practice mindfulness. Another study published in the journal *Obesity Reviews* discovered that mindful eating interventions were successful at promoting weight loss and decreasing binge eating behaviors.

Practical Steps to Begin Mindful Eating

1. Slow Down: One of the simplest methods to begin practicing mindful eating is to slow down when eating. Take small bites, chew thoroughly, and rest your fork between bites.

2. Eliminate Distractions: Try to eat away from distractions like television, smartphones, and computers. Concentrate exclusively on the act of eating and the sensations of each bite.

3. Activate Your Senses: Pay close attention to the colors, smells, textures, and flavors of your food. Take time to enjoy the sensory experience of each bite.

4. Check-In with Your Body: Prior to eating, take time to check in with your body. Are you actually hungry, or are you eating due to boredom, stress, or habit? Throughout the meal, check in on your hunger and fullness levels.

5. Practice Gratitude: Prior to eating, take a moment to express gratitude for your food. This can be a silent acknowledgement or a simple thank you for the food you're about to get.

Starting a mindful eating practice can be difficult, especially if we are used to eating rapidly and mindlessly. Here are some common obstacles and how to overcome them:

1. Eating on the Go: With our hectic schedules, it can be challenging to find time to sit down for a mindful meal. Try to set out even a few minutes to sit and eat without interruptions. If you have to eat on the go, chew gently and pay attention to the flavors and textures of your meal.

2. Emotional Eating: When we are stressed or distressed, we often turn to food for solace. Recognising emotional eating patterns is the first step towards addressing them. Identify the underlying emotions that are driving your eating and seek other coping strategies, such as talking to a friend, practicing deep breathing, or indulging in a pastime.

3. Judgment and Guilt: It is typical to feel guilty or judged for our eating habits. Remember that mindful eating entails observing without judgment. Be nice to yourself and recognise that occasional excesses are OK.

Mindful Eating in Everyday Life

Mindful eating is not confined to meals; it can be applied to many parts of everyday living. Here are some strategies for incorporating mindful eating into your daily practice.

1. Mindful Snacking: Apply mindful eating techniques to your snacks as well. Choose nutritious snacks and eat them with focus and mindfulness.

2. Mindful Cooking: Use your senses to prepare food. Consider the colors, fragrances, and textures of the components, and appreciate the process of preparing nutritious food.

3. Mindful supermarket Shopping: Approach your supermarket visits with awareness. Create a list of nutritious foods and be present when selecting fresh vegetables and other goods. Avoid shopping while hungry, as this might lead to impulsive purchases.

4. Mindful Drinking: Practice awareness with your beverages as well. Enjoy the flavor and aroma of your coffee, tea, or water, and note how it makes you feel.

The Transformative Power of Mindful

Mindful eating has the potential to change our relationship with food and improve our general well-being. By cultivating mindfulness and intention in our eating habits, we can find greater satisfaction and delight in our meals while also developing a healthier, more balanced eating style.

As we embark on our mindful eating adventure, let us remember Thich Nhat Hanh, a well-known mindfulness teacher, who said, _"When you eat, just eat."_ This simple yet deep advice reminds us to be completely present and involved in the act of eating, savoring the nutrients and enjoyment it provides.

By embracing mindful eating, we can have a good knock-on impact in all parts of our lives, encouraging more mindfulness, appreciation, and well-being.

Chapter 2:

Developing Awareness in Eating Habits

Eating Awareness is the foundation of mindful eating. It entails being fully present at meals, paying attention to the act of eating, and recognising the indications our bodies and minds provide us. Cultivating awareness can help us make smarter eating choices, enjoy food more, and feel better overall. When we eat mindlessly, we frequently ignore the signals our bodies send, resulting in overeating or making poor dietary choices.

By becoming more conscious of our eating patterns, we may start making deliberate decisions that benefit our health and happiness.

Steps to Increase Awareness

1. Set an Intention: Before you start a meal, take a moment to set your intention. This could be as simple as agreeing to eat slowly or paying attention to your hunger and fullness indicators. Setting an intention helps to focus your attention and guide your dining experience.

2. Create a Pleasant Eating Environment: Select a relaxing and attractive setting to consume your meals. Reduce distractions by turning off the television and putting your phone away. Creating a comfortable environment allows you to concentrate on the act of eating and fully engage your senses.

3. Engage Your Senses: Pay attention to the colors, textures, and scents of your food. Appreciate the effort put into making your food. Engaging your senses improves the dining experience and produces higher satisfaction.

4. Practice Gratitude: Before you take your first mouthful, take a moment to express your appreciation for your food. Consider the path your food took to reach your plate, including the farmers who raised it, the people who delivered it, and the chef who prepared it. Practicing thankfulness can help you connect with your meals and develop a sense of appreciation.

5. Chew deeply: Chewing your food deeply helps with digestion and allows you to properly taste and enjoy it. Try to chew each meal at least 20-30 times, concentrating on the flavors and sensations.

6. Take Breaks: As you eat, take short breaks to check in with your body. Ask yourself if you are still hungry or if you are beginning to feel full. Taking breaks might help you stay tuned into your body's signals and avoid overeating.

7. Reflect on Your Eating Experience: After your meal, take a few seconds to consider your dining experience. Think about how you felt before, during, and after eating. Reflecting on your experience can help you spot patterns and make changes to promote mindful eating in the future.

Identifying Hunger and Fullness Cues

One of the most important components of mindful eating is listening to your body's hunger and fullness cues. Our bodies have the innate ability to regulate food intake, but modern eating habits frequently disturb this natural process.

By being more conscious of these signs, we can learn to eat based on our body's requirements rather than external stimuli.

1. Understanding Hunger: Hunger is the body's indication that it requires sustenance. Physical hunger is commonly manifested as a growling stomach, lightheadedness, or a sense of emptiness. Stress, boredom, and other emotions can all cause emotional hunger. Learning to figure out between physical and emotional hunger is an essential step towards mindful eating.

2. Honoring Fullness: Fullness is the body's method of indicating that it has consumed enough food. It can be described as a feeling of satisfaction and comfort. Listen to your body's signs and stop eating when you're full, even if there's still food on your plate.

3. The Hunger/Fullness Scale: A hunger-fullness scale can be an effective tool for interpreting your body's signals. Before and during meals, score your hunger on a scale of 1 to 10, with 1 representing acute hunger and 10 representing discomforting fullness. Start eating when you are around a 3 or 4 (moderately hungry) and stop when you are around a 7 or 8 (comfortably full).

Emotions and Dating

Emotions influence our eating patterns. Many of us turn to food for comfort when we're stressed, upset, or bored. While eating for emotional reasons is appropriate, using food as a primary coping technique can lead to harmful eating habits.

1. **Identifying Emotional Triggers:** The first step in overcoming emotional eating is identifying your triggers. Keep a notebook to record your eating habits and the feelings you feel before and after meals. Look for trends and common triggers, such as stress, loneliness, or exhaustion.

2. **Building Alternative Coping Strategies:** After you've recognised your emotional triggers, focus on building non-food coping strategies. This could involve going for a stroll, practicing deep breathing, talking to a buddy, or participating in a hobby. Finding healthy ways to deal with emotions will help you avoid relying on food for comfort.

3. **Practicing Self-Compassion:** Instead of passing judgment, approach emotional eating with compassion. Recognise that turning to food for consolation is a common and normal response. Treat yourself with kindness and tolerance as you seek to create healthy coping strategies.

Mindful Eating Exercises

Mindful eating exercises can help you gain more awareness and strengthen your eating habits. Here are some exercises you might try:

1. **The Raisin activity:** In this classic mindful eating activity, you consume a single raisin with

complete mindfulness. Hold the sultana in your palm and examine its texture, color, and shape. Smell the sultana and observe its aroma. Place the sultana in your mouth and chew carefully, focusing on the flavors and sensations. This activity promotes mindfulness and appreciation for the sensory experience of eating.

2. Body Scan Before Meals: Before you start eating, do a quick body scan. Sit quietly and focus your attention on different parts of your body, noting any feelings of hunger, stress, or discomfort. This technique might help you become more aware of your body's signals and cultivate a sense of presence before meals.

3. Mindful Meal: Choose one meal per day and eat it deliberately from beginning to end. During this meal, avoid all distractions and concentrate only on the act of eating. Engage your senses, eat carefully, and stay in touch with your body throughout the meal. After your experience, reflect on any observations or insights you gained.

4. Gratitude Practice: Add gratitude practice to your mealtime routine. Before you eat, take a moment to express thanks, either silently or verbally, for your meal, the people who prepared it, and the nourishment it gives. Practicing thankfulness can increase your appreciation for your meals and provide a more enjoyable eating experience.

Quotes About Mindful Eating

Incorporating insights from mindfulness professionals can inspire and guide you on your path to mindful eating. Here are some quotes to think about:

1. Thich Nhat Hanh: *"When you eat, just eat."* This simple suggestion from the renowned mindfulness teacher urges us to be fully present and engaged while eating.

2. Jon Kabat-Zinn: *"Mindfulness is paying attention in a particular way: on purpose, in the present moment, and non-judgmentally."* Applying this definition to eating can help us develop more awareness and acceptance.

3. Geneen Roth states, *"Awareness is learning to keep yourself company."* This quote emphasizes the value of being present with oneself and our experiences, including our eating habits.

4. Evelyn Tribole and Elyse Resch: *"Respect your hunger. "Respect your fullness."*

Making Lasting Change

Cultivating awareness in eating behaviors is a lifetime process that requires effort and patience. Here are some tips for creating long-term change:

1. Begin modest: Instead of attempting to remodel your entire eating regimen all at once, start with modest, doable modifications. Choose one or two mindful eating habits to work on each week.

2. Be Consistent: Consistency is essential while adopting new behaviors. Aim to practice mindful eating on a regular basis, even if it's just one meal or snack per day.

3. Seek Support: Tell your friends and family about your mindful eating journey so they may offer you encouragement and support. Consider attending a mindful eating group or consulting with a mindfulness coach or therapist.

4. Reflect and Adjust: Review your mindful eating habits on a regular basis and make any necessary changes. Identify what works effectively and what problems you have, and be willing to make changes to help you achieve your goals.

5. Celebrate Progress: Acknowledge your accomplishments and progress along the road. Recognise the beneficial adjustments you're making and how they affect your well-being.

Cultivating awareness in your eating habits is an effective method to improve your connection with food and general well-being. Paying attention to the present moment, engaging your senses, and listening to your body's signals allows you to make deliberate choices that promote your health and pleasure. Remember that mindful eating is about practice rather than perfection.

Each meal presents an opportunity to practice mindfulness and make decisions that are consistent with your values and aspirations. Accept the trip with an open heart and mind, and experience the transformative power of mindful eating. As you continue down this path, may your meals bring you more happiness and delight, as well as a stronger connection with your body and mind.

Chapter 3:

Mindful Living

The Relationship Between Mindfulness and Emotional Balance Mindful living extends beyond the dining table and into all facets of our everyday life.

At its foundation, mindful living is about being present, aware, and deliberate in our actions, thoughts, and emotions. This strategy can dramatically improve our emotional equilibrium, resulting in better mental health, less stress, and a more fulfilling existence.

In today's fast-paced world, many of us experience emotional turmoil. We frequently react quickly to pressures, feel overwhelmed by our responsibilities, and struggle with anxiety and mood swings.

Mindfulness is a great antidote to these issues because it helps us build a sense of calm, clarity, and balance.

Understanding Emotional Balance.

Emotional balance is the ability to regulate our emotions in a healthy and adaptable manner. It does not imply repressing or disregarding our feelings, but rather accepting and responding to them with knowledge and compassion.

Achieving emotional balance includes:

1. Awareness: Recognising and understanding our feelings as they occur.
2. Acceptance: Allowing yourself to experience feelings without judgment.
3. Regulation: Responding to our emotions in a way that promotes our well-being.

The Importance of Mindfulness in Emotional Balance

Mindfulness is essential for promoting emotional balance because it helps us become more aware of our emotions and build healthy reactions to them. Here are a few ways mindfulness might help with emotional balance:

1. Increased Self-Awareness: Mindfulness allows us to tune into our emotions, thoughts, and physical sensations. This increased awareness enables us to identify emotional patterns and triggers, providing useful insights into our emotional landscape.

2. Improved Emotional Regulation: Practicing mindfulness teaches us to observe our feelings without reacting to them. This pause allows for more thinking and measured answers, which reduces impulsive behavior and promotes emotional stability.

3. Greater Compassion: Mindfulness promotes self-compassion, allowing us to treat ourselves with love and understanding during challenging situations. This empathetic attitude can help to reduce the harsh self-criticism that typically comes with emotional suffering.

4. Stress Reduction: Mindfulness activities like meditation and deep breathing trigger the body's relaxation response, which reduces stress and promotes calm. Lower stress levels promote emotional balance.

Effective Mindfulness

Techniques for Emotional Balance To create emotional balance through mindfulness, consider implementing the following practices into your everyday routine.

1. Mindful Breathing: Mindful breathing is a simple but effective practice that entails attention to the breath. Take a few moments each day to sit quietly and focus on your breath as it goes in and out. Observe the feelings of breathing without attempting to change them. Mindful breathing can assist to relax the mind and center your emotions.

2. Body Scan Meditation: This technique entails drawing attention to various parts of the body and noting any sensations, tension, or discomfort.

Spend a few moments focusing on each location, beginning with your toes and progressing to your head. The body scan meditation can help you reconnect with your body and relieve physical and emotional stress.

3. Mindful Observation: Select an object, such as a flower or a candle, and focus your complete attention on it for a few minutes. Examine the colors, shapes, textures, and other characteristics. Mindful observation promotes attention and presence, minimizing mental clutter and increasing emotional clarity.

4. Loving Kindness Meditation: This practice entails cultivating feelings of compassion and love for oneself and others. Begin silently repeating statements like, "May I be happy, healthy, and safe." Gradually extend your wishes to others, including loved ones and even others with whom you disagree. Loving-kindness meditation promotes empathy and emotional warmth.

5. Journaling: Writing down your ideas and feelings can be a therapeutic technique to work with emotions. Set aside time every day to journal about your experiences, emotions, and thoughts. Journaling can reveal insights into your emotional patterns and help you gain a better understanding of yourself.

Bringing Mindfulness into Everyday Life

Mindful living isn't just for formal practices; it can be incorporated into ordinary activities. Here are some suggestions for adding mindfulness into your daily practice.

1. Thoughtful Morning Routine: Begin the day with awareness by devoting a few minutes to a thoughtful practice like meditation, breathing exercises, or setting daily intentions. This might help you start the day on a positive note and approach it with more clarity and balance.

2. Mindful Eating: As previously noted, mindful eating entails fully focusing on the eating experience. Practice mindful eating by savoring each bite and paying attention to your hunger and fullness indicators.

3. Mindful Movement: Add awareness to physical activities like walking, yoga, or stretching. Pay attention to your body's sensations, movement rhythms, and breathing. Mindful exercise can improve the mind-body connection and promote physical and emotional health.

4. attentive Listening: Engage in attentive listening in your relationships with others. Pay complete attention to the person speaking, without interrupting or planning your response. Mindful listening can help you communicate better, build stronger connections, and develop empathy.

5. Mindful Work: Practice mindfulness at work by focusing on one activity at a time and taking frequent breaks to check in with your body and mind. Avoid multitasking, as it might increase stress and decrease effectiveness. Mindful work techniques can increase productivity and prevent burnout.

Overcoming Challenges in Mindful Living

Adopting a mindful lifestyle can be difficult, particularly in a world full of distractions and pressures. Here are some common obstacles and how to solve them:

1. Busy Schedules: Making time for mindfulness might be tough in a hectic schedule. Begin with simple, achievable techniques like mindful breathing or a brief body scan. As you become more comfortable with your mindfulness activities, gradually increase the duration and frequency.

2. Restlessness and Distraction: It is normal to feel restless and distracted during mindfulness

exercises. When this happens, gently return your focus to the current moment, without judgment. Remember that mindfulness is a practice, and it's fine to have wandering thoughts
.

3. Emotional Discomfort: Mindfulness can occasionally elicit uncomfortable emotions. Approach these feelings with curiosity and kindness, allowing yourself to feel them rather than pushing them away. Consider receiving help from a therapist or mindfulness coach if necessary.

4. Perfectionism: Let go of the belief that mindfulness must be practiced flawlessly. There is no right or incorrect method to practice mindfulness. Concentrate on the process rather than the outcome, and acknowledge your accomplishments and development.

Inspirational Quotes About Mindful Living

Reflecting on quotes from mindfulness and well-being professionals can help motivate and guide you on your journey. Here are some quotes to encourage your mindful living practice:

1. Jon Kabat-Zinn says, "*You can't stop the waves, but you can learn to surf.*" This proverb reminds us that, while we cannot control life's obstacles, we can learn to navigate them mindfully and gracefully.

2. Pema Chödrön: "You are the sky. *"Everything else is just the weather."* This remark emphasizes that our fundamental essence is limitless and everlasting, although our thoughts and feelings are fleeting experiences.

3. Eckhart Tolle says, *"Realize deeply that the present moment is all you ever have. "Make the Now your primary focus in life."* This quote urges us to live in the present moment and find serenity within it.

4. Sharon Salzberg: *"Mindfulness is not difficult; we simply need to remember to do it."* This quotation emphasizes how mindfulness is a simple discipline that takes continual effort and memory.

Developing a Mindful

Living Plan Create a personalized mindfulness plan to help you on your journey to mindful living. Here are several ways to get started:

1. Set Clear Intentions: Identify your goals for bringing mindfulness into your life. Consider which areas you wish to prioritize, such as stress reduction, emotional balance, or better relationships.

2. Choose Mindful Practices: Choose mindfulness practices that appeal to you and fit into your schedule. Begin with a few techniques and progressively build your mindfulness toolset.

3. Schedule Mindfulness Time: Set aside particular hours in your day for mindfulness practices. Developing a long-term mindfulness programme requires consistency.

4. Track Your Progress: Maintain a mindfulness diary to record your practices, reflections, and any changes in your emotional well-being. Reviewing your progress can bring both motivation and insights.

5. Adjust as Needed: Be adaptable and willing to modify your mindfulness plan as necessary. Life is dynamic, and your mindfulness practices should evolve to meet your changing needs and circumstances.

Mindful living is a powerful way to achieve emotional balance and overall well-being. By cultivating mindfulness and presence in our daily lives, we can deal with life's obstacles more easily and resiliently. Mindfulness helps us gain a better awareness of ourselves, improves emotional regulation, and fosters compassion and empathy.

As you begin your path of mindful living, keep in mind that it is an ongoing practice that evolves with time. Approach it with curiosity, patience, and an open heart. Every moment presents an opportunity to practice mindfulness and lead a more balanced, fulfilling life.

Chapter 4: Recognising and Managing Mood and Anxiety

An Introduction to Mood and Anxiety Mood and anxiety problems are common challenges that many people confront throughout their lives. They can have a substantial impact on a person's quality of life, both mentally and physically. Understanding and resolving these diseases via mindful living can lead to helpful techniques for symptom management and relief.

Understanding Mood Disorders

Mood disorders include depression, bipolar disorder, and dysthymia. These illnesses have an emotional impact on people, sometimes resulting in persistent sorrow, anger, or mood swings.

1. **Depression:** Depression is characterized by chronic sorrow, lack of interest in activities, and a variety of physical and cognitive symptoms that can severely impair everyday functioning.

2. **Bipolar Disorder:** Symptoms include significant mood swings, such as mania or hypomania, and depression.

3. **Dysthymia:** A chronic form of depression with less severe but more persistent symptoms than major depressive disorder.

Understanding Anxiety Disorders

Anxiety disorders are characterized by excessive fear or worry, which interferes with regular tasks. Common anxiety disorders include generalized anxiety disorder (GAD), panic disorder, social anxiety disorder, and specific phobias.

1. **Generalized Anxiety Disorder (GAD):** is characterized by excessive, uncontrollable concern

about numerous elements of life, which causes physical symptoms such as restlessness, exhaustion, and muscle tension.

2. Panic Disorder: Consists of recurring panic attacks, which are sudden periods of acute terror accompanied by physical symptoms such as a racing heart, shortness of breath, and dizziness.

3. Social Anxiety Disorder: Excessive dread of social situations and being assessed or scrutinized by others, which causes avoidance of such circumstances.

4. Certain Phobias: are irrational phobias of certain objects or circumstances, such as heights, spiders, or flying.

The Role of Mindfulness in Managing Mood and Anxiety

Mindfulness can be an effective approach for addressing mood and anxiety disorders. It teaches people how to be more conscious of their thoughts and feelings, how to respond to stress in a healthier way, and how to find peace and balance.

1. **Enhanced Self-Awareness:** Mindfulness techniques teach people to notice their thoughts and feelings without judgment. This increased self-awareness can aid in identifying triggers and trends in mood and anxiety.

2. **Emotion Regulation:** Mindfulness helps manage emotions by separating stimuli and response. This promotes more thinking and less reactive behavior, lowering the intensity of emotional experiences.

3. **Stress Reduction:** Mindfulness activities like meditation and deep breathing engage the parasympathetic nervous system, which promotes relaxation and reduces the physiological symptoms of stress and anxiety.

4. **Improved Cognitive Function:** Regular mindfulness meditation can improve cognitive flexibility, attention, and memory, which are frequently hindered in mood and anxiety disorders.

Effective Mindfulness

Techniques for Mood and Anxiety Incorporating mindfulness into daily life can be especially effective for controlling mood and anxiety. Here are a few practical techniques:

1. **Mindful Breathing:** Concentrate on your breath, feeling the sensation of air entering and

exiting your body. If your mind wanders, softly return your attention to your breathing. This exercise can help you stay focused on the present moment and lessen worry.

2. Body Scan Meditation: Lie down or sit comfortably and focus your attention on various parts of your body, beginning with your toes and progressing up to your head. Observe any sensations, tension, or discomfort. This technique can help to relieve bodily stress and promote calm.

3. Mindful Movement: Practice yoga, tai chi, or walking meditation. Focus on your body's actions and sensations to help you stay grounded and lessen tension.

4. Loving-Kindness Meditation: By quietly repeating statements like "May I be happy, may I be healthy, may I be safe," you can generate sentiments of compassion and love for yourself and others. Extend these wishes to others, even if you disagree with them. This technique can improve emotional well-being while decreasing negative feelings.

5. Journaling: Record your ideas, emotions, and experiences. This can aid in emotional processing and provide insights into your mood and anxiety patterns.

Addressing Specific Triggers and Situations.

Recognising and addressing particular causes for mood and anxiety might help people manage their symptoms more effectively.

1. Identifying Trigger: Keep a journal of your mood and anxiety levels, noting any patterns or triggers. Triggers might be situations, people, or stressors.

2. Developing Coping techniques: Once triggers have been identified, create coping techniques to manage them. This could involve using mindfulness techniques, seeking social support, or participating in activities that promote relaxation and well-being.

3. Setting limits: Learn how to create appropriate limits to safeguard your emotional well-being. This could include declining more tasks, avoiding exposure to stressful situations, or prioritizing self-care.

4. Seeking specialist Help: If your symptoms are persistent or severe, consult a mental health specialist. Therapy, medicine, or a combination of the two can be useful in treating mood and anxiety problems.

The Effect of Lifestyle on Emotional Balance

A comprehensive approach to controlling mood and anxiety takes into account lifestyle aspects such as nutrition, exercise, sleep, and social interactions.

1. Diet: A well-balanced diet high in fruits, vegetables, whole grains, and lean proteins helps improve mental health. Avoid excessive caffeine, sugar, and processed meals, which can worsen mood and anxiety problems.

2. Exercise: Regular physical activity produces endorphins, which are natural mood boosters. Aim for 30 minutes of moderate activity most days of the week.

3. Sleep: Prioritize good sleep hygiene by sticking to a consistent sleep schedule, creating a relaxing sleep environment, and avoiding stimulants before bedtime. Adequate sleep is essential for emotional stability and well-being.

4. Social Connections: Strong social support can protect against stress and boost emotional well-being. Maintain regular touch with friends and family, and look for supporting networks or groups.

Quotes to Inspire and Guide

Incorporating advice from mindfulness and mental health specialists can provide motivation and direction. Here are some quotes to think about:

1. **Thich Nhat Hanh** says, "*The present moment is filled with joy and happiness.*" "*If you pay attention, you will notice it.*"

2. **Jon Kabat-Zinn** says, "*You can't stop the waves, but you can learn to surf.*"

3. **Pema Chödrön**: "*You are the sky.* "*Everything else is just the weather.*"

4. **Rumi**: "*The wound is the place where the Light enters you.*"

5. **Sharon Salzberg**: "*Mindfulness is not difficult; we simply need to remember to do it.*"

Developing a Personal Mindfulness

Plan Consider developing a personalized mindfulness approach to effectively manage mood and anxiety. Here's a step-by-step instructions:

1. Set Clear Goals: Define your mood and anxiety management. Be explicit about your goals, such as reducing panic attacks, improving mood stability, or increasing emotional resilience.

2. Choose Mindful Practices: Choose mindfulness practices that appeal to you and fulfill your individual requirements. Begin with a few practices and progressively build your repertory.

3. Schedule Regular Practice: Set aside certain hours in your day for mindfulness practices. Consistency is essential to reaping the advantages of mindfulness.

4. Track Your Progress: Keep a notebook to track your mindfulness activities and how they affect your mood and anxiety. Make note of any changes or enhancements that occur over time.

5. Seek Support: Discuss your mindfulness journey with friends, family, or a support group. Consider working with a mindfulness coach or therapist to improve your practice.

Recognizing and resolving mood and anxiety through mindful living is a highly effective way to improve emotional well-being. Individuals can gain more emotional balance and resilience by improving awareness, emotion regulation skills, and healthy coping techniques. Remember, mindfulness is an ongoing practice that demands patience and dedication.

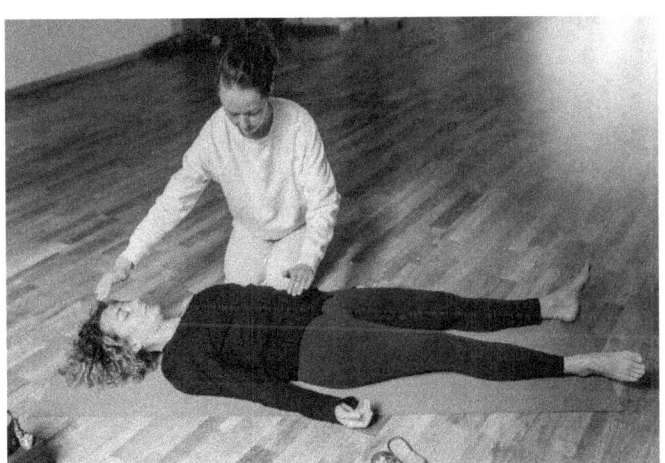

Chapter 5:

Create a Mindful Eating Plan

Mindful eating entails paying complete attention to the act of eating and appreciating your food. It promotes awareness of hunger and fullness cues, as well as a positive relationship with food. Creating a mindful eating plan can help people make more deliberate food choices, improve digestion, and improve their general well-being.

Principles of Mindful Eating

To develop a mindful eating plan, you must first comprehend the fundamental concepts of mindful eating. These concepts provide the framework for making more conscientious and nutritious dietary choices.

1. Awareness: Being fully present throughout meals, focusing on the flavors, textures, and scents of the food.

2. Non-judgment: Approaching food without labeling it "good" or "bad," and avoiding the guilt or shame that comes with eating.

3. Listening to Your Body: Using bodily hunger and fullness signals to influence food choices.

4. Savoring: Taking the time to savor and enjoy each bite, enabling oneself to feel the delight of eating.

5. Thankfulness: Developing a sense of thankfulness for the food and the nutrition it offers.

Steps to Create a Mindful Eating Plan

Developing a mindful eating strategy requires several steps. These stages will help you set objectives, make dietary choices, and integrate mindfulness into your eating habits.

1. Set Clear Goals: Determine your aims for mindful eating. Do you want to improve digestion, lose weight, minimize emotional eating, or just enjoy your food more? Setting specific goals will help you maintain focus and motivation.

2. Evaluate Your Current Eating Habits: Consider your existing eating routines. Do you frequently eat while distracted? Do you understand your hunger and fullness cues? Understanding your starting point will allow you to find areas for progress.

3. Plan Balanced Meals: Strive for balanced meals that contain a variety of nutrients. Incorporate entire grains, lean proteins, healthy fats, and a variety of fruits and vegetables. A well-balanced diet promotes general health and wellness.

4. Create a Structured Eating Schedule: Set aside regular meal and snack times to help regulate appetite and avoid overeating. Consistent eating patterns can help to control blood sugar levels and prevent cravings.

5. Set Up Mindful Eating Spaces: Designate specific eating places that are distraction-free. Create a relaxing and attractive environment that promotes mindful eating.

6. **Practice Mindful Eating ways:** Use particular ways to improve mindfulness when eating. These tactics include eating deliberately, savoring every bite, and paying attention to hunger and fullness cues.

7. **Reflect and Adjust:** Review your mindful eating habits on a regular basis and make any necessary changes. Maintaining a long-term mindful eating strategy requires flexibility and self-compassion.

Creating Clear Goals for Mindful Eating

Setting specific and attainable goals is the first step towards creating a mindful eating strategy. Consider short-term and long-term goals that are consistent with your overall health and well-being.

Short-Term Goals: - Eat one mindful meal every day. - Minimize distractions during meals, such as turning off the television or putting your phone aside. - Practice mindful breathing before beginning a meal.

Long-term Goals: - Establish a mindful eating practice. - Improve digestion and alleviate digestive discomfort. - Develop a pleasant relationship with food and avoid emotional eating.

Assessing Your Current Eating Habits

To develop an effective mindful eating strategy, you should first examine your present eating patterns. Consider maintaining a food diary for a week to chart your eating habits, including what you eat, when you eat, and how you feel before and after each meal.

Questions to Consider:

Do you frequently eat on-the-go or while multitasking? -

How often do you eat due to boredom, stress, or other emotions? -

Do you eat until you're too full, or do you stop when you're satisfied? -

Are there certain times of day when you are more likely to overeat or make poor eating decisions?

Plan Balanced Meals

A mindful eating plan should include well-balanced meals that contain vital nutrients. Aim to include a variety of food types to ensure you are getting enough vitamins, minerals, and other nutrients. A balanced meal includes healthy grains such as brown rice, quinoa, whole wheat bread, and oats, which give fibre and lasting energy.

Lean Proteins: Chicken, fish, beans, lentils, and tofu all promote muscular health and satiety.

Healthy Fats: Avocados, nuts, seeds, and olive oil improve heart health and aid in the absorption of fat-soluble vitamins.

Fruits and Vegetables: Choose a diversity of colours to acquire a wide spectrum of antioxidants and nutrients.

Hydration: Drink enough of water throughout the day to improve your digestion and general health

Developing a Structured Eating Schedule

A planned eating routine can help you control your hunger and avoid overeating. Plan regular meals and snacks to keep your energy levels up and prevent impulsive eating.

Meal Period	Time	Type of Meal
Beakfast	7.00AM	Morning Snack
Lunch	1.00 PM	Afternoon Snacks
Dinner	7.00 PM	Evening Snacks

Setting Up Mindful Eating Spaces

Your eating environment might have a significant impact on your eating habits. Make a mindful dining environment devoid of distractions and conducive to relaxation and enjoyment.

Tips for Mindful Eating Spaces:

Minimize Distractions: Create a serene and quiet setting by turning off the TV and putting away technological devices.

Prepare the Table: To provide a comfortable meal experience, use placemats, napkins, and appropriate cutlery.

Focus on Meals: Sit down to eat, even if it's just a snack, and avoid standing or strolling around.

Practice Mindful Eating Techniques

Incorporate particular practices for increasing mindfulness during meals. These techniques can help you become more conscious of your eating habits and enjoy your meals more thoroughly.

1. Eat Slowly: Take tiny portions and chew well. Eating slowly allows you to savor the flavors and textures of your food while also giving your body enough time to signal satiety.

2. Savor Each Bite: Concentrate on the sensory experience of eating, such as the flavor, aroma, and texture of your food. Take the time to appreciate and relish every bite.

3. Pay Attention to Hunger and Fullness Signals: Be aware of your body's hunger and fullness indicators. Eat when you are hungry and quit when you are content but not overly full.

4. Engage All Your Senses: Pay attention to the colors, forms, and presentation of your food. Engaging all of your senses can improve the eating experience and boost enjoyment.

5. Practice thanks: Before eating, take a moment to express thanks for your meal, the effort put into preparing it, and the sustenance it gives.

Reflecting and Adjusting Your Plan

Mindful eating is a continuous discipline that necessitates frequent reflection and correction. Periodically evaluate your mindful eating strategy to discover what works effectively and where there is potential for improvement.

- How does mindful eating affect your physical and emotional well-being? -

-Are there any times or situations where mindful eating is difficult? -

-What changes can you make to support your mindful eating goals?

Inspirational Quotes About Mindful Eating

Experts and thinkers' insight can inspire and encourage you on your mindful eating journey. Here are some quotes to think about:

1. Thich Nhat Hanh: "*Drink your tea slowly and reverently, as if it is the axis on which the world earth revolves - slowly, evenly, without rushing towards the future.*"

2. **Michael Pollan** *says, "Eat food." Not too much. Mostly plants.*

3. **Buddha**: *"In the end, just three things matter: How well we have lived, how well we have loved, how well we have learned to let go."*

4. **Jon Kabat-Zinn:** *"When you pay attention to your thoughts, you notice that they are frequently the same thoughts you had yesterday, the day before, and the day before that." "They're like whispering to yourself."*

Creating a mindful eating plan is a step towards a healthier and more satisfying relationship with food. Setting clear goals, reviewing your present habits, planning balanced meals, building an organized eating schedule, creating mindful eating spaces, practicing specific skills, and reflecting on your progress on a regular basis will help you cultivate a sustainable and nourishing eating lifestyle.

Mindful eating encourages you to slow down, enjoy your meals, and pay attention to your body's demands. It promotes a stronger connection with the present moment and improves your general well-being. Remember that mindfulness is a practice that evolves with time. Begin your mindful eating journey with curiosity, patience, and self-compassion.

Chapter 6: Nurturing the Body and Mind with Intention

Nourishing the body and mind with intention entails more than just eating food to support life. It entails making aware food choices and eating habits that promote both physical and emotional well-being. This chapter discusses how to develop a stronger relationship with your food, recognise its benefits, and incorporate this mindful practice into your daily life.

The concept of nourishment

Nourishment is more than just giving the body calories; it also includes nutrients that support maximum health and well-being. Mindful nourishment takes into account the quality of the food, the nutritional balance, and the setting in which it is consumed.

Key Aspects of Nourishment:

1. Nutrient Density: Selecting foods high in vitamins, minerals, and important nutrients.

2. Balance: Providing a diverse range of foods from various food groups to meet all nutritional requirements.

3. Quality: Choose whole, minimally processed meals that preserve their natural nutrients.

The Relationship Between Food and Mood

What we consume has a big impact on our mood and mental health. Certain nutrients and dietary habits are linked to higher mood, reduced stress, and improved cognitive function.

1. Complex Carbohydrates: Whole grains and vegetables help keep blood sugar levels constant, which helps improve mood.

2. Omega-3 Fatty Acids: Found in fatty fish, flaxseeds, and walnuts, these fats are important for brain function and have been related to lower levels of depression and anxiety.

3. B Vitamins: These vitamins, which may be found in leafy greens, legumes, and whole grains, are essential for brain function and the generation of neurotransmitters that regulate mood.

4. Antioxidants: Antioxidant-rich fruits and vegetables can help protect the brain from oxidative stress, a risk factor for mood disorders.

Mindful Eating Physical Health

Mindful eating ensures that the body gets the nutrition it requires by encouraging thoughtful meal choices and improving the eating experience.

1. Listening to Hunger and Fullness Cues: Using your body's cues to decide when and how much to eat.

2. Choosing Nutrient-Rich Foods: Choosing foods that provide a variety of vital elements to support bodily functioning.

3. Portion Control: Keeping track of portion proportions to avoid overeating and maintain a healthy weight.

Strategies for Intentional Nourishment

Using purposeful feeding in your daily life necessitates various practical tactics. These techniques aid in making mindful eating a constant and lasting practice.

1. Meal Planning: Planning meals ahead of time will help you maintain a balanced diet and avoid impulsive, unhealthy food choices.

2. Mindful Grocery Shopping: Creating a list of nutrient-dense items and sticking to it when shopping can help promote healthy eating habits.

3. Cooking at Home: Preparing meals at home gives you more control over the materials and serving amounts.

Meal Planning With Intention

Meal planning is an effective technique for conscious nourishment. It enables you to make conscious food choices and maintains a balanced and nutritious diet.

Steps to Effective Meal Planning:

1. Set Specific Goals: Determine your nutritional objectives, such as increasing vegetable consumption or minimizing processed foods.

2. Create a Weekly Menu: Plan your meals and snacks for the week, including a variety of dietary categories.

3. Make a Shopping List: List all of the ingredients you'll need for your scheduled meals to avoid making unnecessary purchases.

4. Prep Ahead: To save time and stress during the week, prepare ingredients or full meals ahead of time.

Mindful Grocery Shopping

Grocery shopping with intention is making deliberate choices about what foods to purchase. It helps to ensure that your kitchen is stocked with nutritious foods that support your health goals.

Advice for Mindful Grocery Shopping:

1. Shop the Perimeter: Concentrate on the store's exterior aisles, which often contain fresh fruit, meats, and dairy products.

2. Read Labels: Use ingredient lists and nutritional information to make informed decisions.

3. Avoid Shopping While Hungry: Shopping on an empty stomach can result in impulsive purchases of harmful items.

4. Support Local and Seasonal: Whenever feasible, buy fresher, more nutritious produce grown locally or seasonally.

Cooking and eating mindfully

Cooking and eating at home allows you to completely participate in the process of creating and consuming meals. This can improve both the eating experience and the nutritional value of your meals.

1. Thoughtful Cooking: Treat cooking as a thoughtful exercise, focusing on the sensory experiences involved, such as slicing vegetables, stirring a pot, or smelling spices.

2. Eating atmosphere: Set up a peaceful, distraction-free mealtime atmosphere. Set the table, turn down the lights, and play quiet music if it improves your dining experience.

3. Savoring Each Bite: Take the time to chew properly and enjoy the flavors and textures of your food.

The role of hydration

Maintaining proper hydration is an essential component of mindful nutrition. Water is required for several body activities, such as digestion, nutrition absorption, and temperature regulation.

Tips to Stay Hydrated:

1. Drink Water Regularly: Aim for at least eight glasses of water every day, with adjustments dependent on activity level and weather.

2. Bring a Water Bottle: Carry a reusable water bottle with you to encourage consistent hydration throughout the day.

3. Eat Water-Rich Foods: Consume foods high in water content, such as cucumbers, tomatoes, and watermelons.

Emotional and Social Aspects of Eating

Eating is a physical, emotional, and social event. Mindful eating entails recognising and treating the emotional components of eating, as well as encouraging pleasant food-related social interactions.

1. Emotional Eating: Recognise triggers for emotional eating and devise healthy coping mechanisms, such as mindfulness or physical activity.

2. Social Connections: Share meals with family and friends to increase your pleasure of eating and strengthen social relationships.

3. Cultural and Family customs: Celebrate cultural and family food customs to foster a sense of identity and belonging.

Quotes to Encourage Mindful Nourishment

Incorporating the wisdom of others can bring inspiration and guidance on your path to mindful nutrition. Here are some quotes to think about:

1. Michael Pollan: *"Eat food, but not too much, and mostly plants."*

2. Hippocrates *said, "Let food be thy medicine and medicine be thy food."*

3. Alice Waters: *"The table is a meeting place, a gathering ground, the source of sustenance and nourishment, festivity, safety, and satisfaction."*

4. Dalai Lama: *"Approach love and cooking with reckless abandon."*

Practical Exercises for Mindful Nourishment

Incorporate these practical exercises into your routine to improve mindful eating.

1. Mindful Eating Meditation: Before each meal, take a few moments to breathe deeply and center yourself. Concentrate on your future meal and set a goal for mindful eating.

2. Gratitude Practice: Before eating, express your appreciation for the food and the effort that went into its preparation. This can help you appreciate and enjoy the dish.

3. Mindful Food notebook: Keep a notebook to record your eating patterns, including what you eat, when you eat, and how you feel before and after meals. This can assist uncover trends and areas for improvement.

Nourishing the body and mind with intention is a comprehensive method that takes into account the quality, balance, and emotional elements of eating. Setting clear goals, planning meals, shopping thoughtfully, cooking at home, and having a supportive eating environment can all help you develop a healthier and more enjoyable relationship with food.

Note that mindful nutrition is a continuous practice that evolves with time. Approach it with curiosity, patience, and self-compassion, and enjoy the road to better health and well-being.

Chapter 7: Strategies to Overcome Emotional Eating

Emotional eating is when people eat to cope with their emotions rather than to relieve their physical hunger. This behavior can perpetuate a cycle of guilt, humiliation, and unhealthy eating behaviors. Understanding emotional eating and devising techniques to combat it is critical for cultivating a healthier relationship with food and reaching overall well-being.

Understanding Emotional Eating.

Stress, anxiety, melancholy, or boredom are common triggers for emotional eating. It is also linked to good feelings, such as eating to celebrate. The key is to recognise that emotional eating is motivated not by physical hunger, but by a desire to soothe or improve emotional emotions.

Common Triggers for Emotional Eating:

1. Stress: Excessive stress might cause desires for sugary and fattening comfort foods.

2. Boredom: Eating can become a way to pass the time while also providing excitement.

3. Emotional Upset: Eating can be used to self-soothe when you are sad, lonely, or anxious.

4. Celebration: Positive events and celebrations frequently include food, which leads to overeating.

Recognising the Signs of Emotional Eating.

To manage emotional eating, it is critical to recognise the symptoms and distinguish it from real hunger. Emotional hunger usually strikes unexpectedly, is exclusive to certain comfort foods, and is not satiated by a full stomach.

Signs of Emotional Eating:

1. Sudden Cravings: Strong cravings that appear unexpectedly, particularly for certain comfort foods.

2. Mindless Eating: eating without paying attention to the food or your body's cues.

3. Unrelated to Physical Hunger: Eating when you are not actually hungry.

4. Emotional Triggers: Eating based on emotions rather than hunger.

5. Regret and Guilt: Feeling bad or guilty after eating.

Strategies for Overcoming Emotional

Eating Overcoming emotional eating necessitates self-awareness, alternate coping mechanisms, and mindful eating habits. The following techniques can help you manage your emotions without resorting to food.

1. Develop Self-Awareness: Recognising your emotional triggers and eating habits is the first step towards overcoming emotional eating.

2. Practice Mindfulness: Being present and aware throughout meals can help you identify emotional eating and make more deliberate food choices.

3. Find Alternative Coping Mechanisms: Determine and practice better ways to deal with emotions, such as physical activity, writing, or talking to a friend.

4. Set Food Boundaries: To avoid mindless eating, establish clear boundaries surrounding meal times and routines.

5. Seek Professional Help: Consult with a therapist or counsellor to help you identify the underlying causes of emotional eating and build appropriate coping methods.

Developing Self-Awareness

Self-awareness is essential for identifying the triggers and patterns linked with emotional eating. Keeping a food and mood journal might help you monitor your eating habits and emotions.

Steps to Increase Self-Awareness:

1. Track Your Eating Habits: Keep track of what you eat, when you eat, and how you feel before and after you eat.

2. Identify trends: Look for trends in your journal that point to emotional eating triggers.

3. Reflect on Emotional Triggers: Think about the feelings and situations that lead to emotional eating.

Practice Mindfulness

Mindfulness can help you become more aware of your eating patterns and form a better relationship with food. Mindful eating entails paying close attention to the entire eating experience, from the flavor and texture of the food to the body's hunger and fullness signals.

Tips for Mindful Eating:

1. Eat Slowly: Take your time chewing and savoring each bite, allowing your body to feel full.

2. Eliminate Distractions: Avoid distractions such as television, phones, and other activities when eating.

3. Engage Your Senses: Pay attention to the colors, smells, textures, and flavors of your food.

4. Listen to Your Body: Let your hunger and fullness signals guide your eating.

Identifying Alternative Coping Strategies

Identifying and practicing alternate ways to cope with emotions might help minimise reliance on food for comfort. These choices should address the emotional demands that underpin emotional eating.

Healthy coping strategies:

1. Physical Activity: Exercise can help reduce stress, improve mood, and give a healthy outlet for emotions.

2. Journaling: Writing about your emotions might help you process them and get insight into your current state.

3. Social Support: Speaking with friends, relatives, or a support group can offer emotional support and alleviate feelings of loneliness.

4. Relaxation Techniques: Deep breathing, meditation, and yoga can all help with stress and emotional suffering.

Setting Boundaries With Food

Putting clear limits around food can help prevent emotional eating and promote healthy habits. This entails establishing clear standards for when and how you eat

. Tips for Establishing Boundaries:

1. Scheduled Meals and Snacks: Eat regularly to avoid compulsive eating.

2. Designated Eating places: To create a controlled eating environment, limit your eating to certain places, such as the kitchen or dining room.

3. Healthy Food Choices: Stock your kitchen with healthy options and keep trigger items to a minimum.

4. Portion Control: Serve meals in proper quantity to prevent overeating.

Seeking Professional Support

Professional help from therapists, dietitians, or counselors can be quite beneficial in resolving emotional eating. They can offer tailored advice and solutions to help you manage emotional eating properly.

Types of Professional Support:

1. Therapy: Cognitive-behavioral therapy (CBT) can help you recognise and change the thoughts and behaviors that contribute to emotional eating.

2. Nutrition Counseling: A registered dietician can assist you in developing a balanced food plan and maintaining good eating habits.

3. Support Groups: Joining a support group can provide you a sense of belonging and shared experience, making you feel less alone on your path.

Effective Exercises for Overcoming Emotional

Eating Including practical workouts in your daily routine can help reinforce healthy eating habits and emotional coping methods.

1. Mindful Eating Meditation: Before each meal, take a few moments to breathe deeply and center yourself. Concentrate on your future meal and set a goal for mindful eating.

2. Gratitude Practice: Express gratitude for your food and the effort put into its preparation. This can help you appreciate and enjoy the dish.

3. Stress Reduction Techniques: Deep breathing, gradual muscle relaxation, and mindfulness meditation can all help reduce stress and emotional suffering.

4. Healthy Distractions: Engage in activities that offer healthy alternatives to emotional eating, such as reading, hobbies, or spending time with loved ones.

Inspirational Quotes About Emotional Eating

Reflecting on the wisdom of others might bring inspiration and assistance in overcoming emotional eating. Here are some quotes to encourage you on your journey:

1. **Geneen Roth:** *"Our relationship to food expresses our relationship with ourselves."*

2. **Brenda Brown:** *"We cannot selectively numb emotions; when we numb the painful emotions, we also numb the positive emotions."*

3. **Thich Nhat Hanh:** *"Feelings pass like clouds in a windy sky. Conscious breathing is my anchor."*

4. **Unknown**: *"Hunger is not an emergency."*

Overcoming emotional eating is a process that needs self-awareness, mindfulness, alternate coping skills, and professional assistance. You may improve your general well-being by learning about your emotional triggers, practicing mindful eating, finding healthy ways to cope with emotions, setting food limits, and seeking support.

Passing over emotional eating is a continuous process that requires tolerance, compassion, and perseverance. Approach this path with curiosity and love to yourself, and celebrate every step you make towards improved eating habits and emotional balance.

Chapter 8:

Bringing Mindfulness into Daily Life

Mindfulness is the practice of remaining fully present and engaged in the present moment, free of judgment or distraction. Incorporating mindfulness into daily life can boost awareness, reduce stress, and improve general well-being. This section investigates practical strategies to apply mindfulness into numerous facets of daily life, ranging from routine tasks to difficult situations.

Understanding Mindfulness.

Mindfulness is fundamentally about paying attention to the current moment with openness and curiosity. It entails witnessing ideas, emotions, and experiences without judgment or attachment. Mindfulness practice can help people acquire more clarity, resilience, and compassion in their daily lives.

Benefits of Mindfulness

Mindfulness has numerous benefits for both physical and mental health. These advantages apply to a wide range of aspects of life, including stress reduction, improved attention and concentration, improved emotional control, and increased life satisfaction.

Key Advantages of Mindfulness:

1. Stress Reduction: Mindfulness techniques can lower stress by encouraging calm and offering strategies for dealing with difficult situations.

2. Improved Focus: By teaching the mind to focus on the present moment, mindfulness improves concentration and cognitive performance.

3. Emotional Regulation: Mindfulness techniques enable people to recognise and regulate challenging emotions more effectively, resulting in greater emotional balance.

4. Enhanced Well-Being: Consistent mindfulness practice has been linked to enhanced life satisfaction, happiness, and general well-being.

Practical Approaches to Integrating Mindfulness into Daily Life

Mindfulness may be incorporated into regular tasks without being complex. Simple activities and thoughtful moments throughout the day can help you become more present and aware.
Here are some practical methods to incorporate mindfulness into several elements of your daily life:

1. Thoughtful Morning Routine: - Start each day with a few minutes of thoughtful breathing or meditation.- Pay attention to every aspect of your daily ritual, from cleaning your teeth to preparing breakfast.

2. Mindful Eating: - Enjoy each bite of your food.- Pay attention to the colors, textures, and flavors of the foods you eat.- Eat without distractions, concentrating exclusively on the act of eating.

3. Mindful Movement: - Practice mindful walking by focusing on the sensations of each stride.- Practice yoga, tai chi, or other gentle movements while paying attention to your breathing and body.

4. Mindful Communication: Actively listen to others without interrupting or responding.- Speak thoughtfully, selecting words with care and intention.

5. Mindful Work: Take small mindfulness breaks throughout the day to pause, breathe, and refocus.- Approach activities with complete concentration and focus, one at a time.

6. Mindful Technology Use: Establish boundaries for technology use to avoid mindless browsing or multitasking.- Practice digital awareness by taking breaks from screens and doing offline activities.

7. Mindful Evening Rituals: Relax before bedtime with a relaxing mindfulness practice, like a body scan meditation or gentle stretching.- Reflect on the day with thankfulness, highlighting moments of mindfulness and growth.

Overcoming Common Challenges

While incorporating mindfulness into daily life can be beneficial, it does not come without hurdles. Common challenges include resistance, distractions, and trouble maintaining regularity. Here are some strategies for addressing the challenges:

1. Begin Small: Start with short, manageable mindfulness practices and progressively expand the duration and complexity over time.

2. Find What Works for You: Experiment with several mindfulness practices to see what speaks to you personally.

3. Be Patient and Persistent: Cultivating mindfulness is a lifelong endeavor, so be patient with yourself and commit to consistent practice, especially on days when it feels difficult.

4. Create Reminders: Use signals or triggers throughout the day to remind yourself to pause and practice mindfulness, such as posting sticky notes in visible places or setting phone alarms.

5. Practice Self-Compassion: Approach your mindfulness practice with kindness and self-compassion, knowing that it's normal to experience times of difficulty or distraction.

Developing Mindful Habits

Integrating mindfulness into daily life entails building attentive habits that become natural and effortless over time. Individuals who constantly practice mindfulness in various aspects of their lives might gain better awareness, resilience, and inner serenity.

Tips for Developing Mindful Habits:

1. Set Intentions: Begin each day with a thoughtful intention or aim for how you want to present yourself in the world.

2. Create Rituals: Establish daily mindfulness rituals, such as pausing for a moment of silence before meals or taking a thoughtful walk in nature.

3. Practice Gratitude: Be grateful for the present moment and the small pleasures of daily existence.

4. Stay Curious: Approach mindfulness with curiosity and openness, always seeking new techniques and viewpoints.

5. Connect with Community: Surround yourself with supportive people who share your passion for mindfulness and well-being, and participate in mindfulness activities together.

Inspirational Quotes about Mindfulness

Reflecting on the wisdom of others can motivate and strengthen your mindfulness practice. Here are a few quotes to consider:

1. **Jon Kabat-Zinn** *says, "You can't stop the waves, but you can learn to surf."*

2. **Thich Nhat Hanh**: *"The present moment is the only moment available to us, and it opens the door to all other moments."*

3. **Eckhart Tolle**: *"Realise deeply that the present moment is all you ever have."*

4. **Rumi:** *"The quieter you become, the more you are able to hear."*

Mindfulness into daily life is an effective technique to increase presence, awareness, and well-being. Individuals who include simple mindfulness practices into their daily routines might reduce stress, improve focus, and feel more satisfied with their lives

Remember that mindfulness is a journey, not a destination, and that every moment presents an opportunity to develop deeper awareness and presence. Welcome to a mindfulness-based life, where every moment is an invitation to awaken to the fullness of life. May the practice of mindfulness bring you peace, joy, and fulfilment, enriching every part of your daily life.

Chapter 9: Dealing with Food Cravings and Temptation

Food cravings and temptations are typical occurrences that can derail even the best-intentioned diet regimes. Understanding the root causes of cravings and devising effective techniques to manage them is critical for sustaining healthy eating habits and achieving long-term fitness. In this chapter, we'll look at the science behind food cravings, common triggers, and effective ways to overcome them.

Understanding Food Cravings.

Food cravings are strong urges for certain foods that are typically heavy in sugar, fat, or salt. While cravings might be driven by hunger or physiological needs, they are also frequently impacted by psychological and environmental variables.

Common Reasons for Food Cravings:

1. Emotional Triggers: Stress, boredom, melancholy, and other emotions might cause desires for comfort foods.

2. Habitual Patterns: Repeated behaviors or routines might form links between certain activities and foods.

3. Social Influences: Peer pressure, cultural standards, and social environments can all impact food preferences and cravings.

4. Nutritional Deficiencies: Although less common than other triggers, cravings might be caused by the body's lack of specific nutrients.

Strategies for Managing Food Cravings:

While food cravings might be overwhelming, there are a few ways that can help people control them better. Individuals can minimise the frequency and intensity of cravings by recognising the underlying causes and employing effective measures.

1. Identify Triggers: Be aware of the situations, feelings, or activities that cause cravings. Keeping a journal might help you find patterns and root reasons.

2. Practice Mindful Awareness: When a craving emerges, halt and observe it without judgment. Recognise the need and pay attention to any bodily feelings or emotions it triggers.

3. Distract Yourself: Try a distracting activity to divert your attention away from the urge. This could involve going for a walk, engaging in a pastime, or contacting a buddy.

4. Find Healthy Alternatives: Rather than succumbing to the urge, select a healthy alternative that fulfills the same need. Choose a piece of fruit instead of a sweet snack.

5. Address Underlying requirements: If your desires are caused by emotional or psychological requirements, look at alternative ways to meet them. This could include using relaxation techniques, finding social support, or treating underlying stressors.

6. Practice Moderation: Instead of starving yourself completely, allow yourself to indulge in occasional delights. Restrictive diets are frequently associated with increased desires and, ultimately, overeating.

7. Plan Ahead: Anticipate circumstances when cravings are likely to arise and prepare by keeping healthful foods on hand. This can assist to reduce impulsive behavior and make healthier choices easier.

Mindful Eating for Craving Control

Mindful eating practices can be especially beneficial in managing food cravings since they increase awareness of hunger and fullness cues, reduce mindless eating, and promote healthy eating habits.

1. **Eat Mindfully:** Focus on the sensory experience of eating, such as the taste, texture, and aroma of the meal. Chew slowly and savor every bite.

2. **Check in with Hunger Cues:** Prior to eating, rate your level of hunger on a scale of 1 to 10. Eat when you are moderately hungry (about a 3 or 4), and stop when you are pleasantly full (around a 6 or 7).

3. **Practise the 5 S's**: Before succumbing to a need, pause and consider the following questions: -

**Stop: Pause for a bit and take several deep breaths. -

Scan: Check in with your body to see if you're actually hungry or if the craving is caused by something else.

smell: Take time to sniff the cuisine you want, allowing yourself to absorb the aroma before indulging.

Sip: Drinking a glass of water or herbal tea will help quench thirst and lower the intensity of the appetite.

savor: If you still have a craving after following the preceding steps, allow yourself to eat a little piece mindfully, focusing on each bite and ending when you're full.

Dealing with Temptations

In addition to managing food cravings, people may face temptations in their surroundings that make it difficult to stick to their health goals. Here are some techniques to deal with temptations:

1. Modify Your Environment: Keep enticing meals out of sight or reach. Instead, fill your environment with healthy options that help you achieve your goals.

2. Practice Self-Regulation: Improve your self-control by incorporating tactics like delayed gratification, diversion, and reframing thoughts about temptation.

3. Establish Clear Boundaries: Create clear rules or guidelines for partaking in enticing meals, such as permitting oneself a small portion on rare occasions or restricting particular foods to once a week.

4. Seek Support: Enlist the help of friends, family, or a support group to keep you accountable and manage difficult situations.

Quotes that Inspire Resilience

Drawing on the advice of others can provide motivation and strength when dealing with food cravings and temptations. Here are some quotes to think about:

1. **Buddha** *says, "The mind is everything." "What you think, you become."*

2. **Eleanor Roosevelt:** *"You must do the thing you think you cannot do."*

3. **Confucius:** *"It does not matter how slowly you go as long as you do not stop."*

4. **Maya Angelou:** *"You may encounter many defeats, but you must not be defeated."*

Managing food cravings and temptations is a continuous process that needs self-awareness, mindfulness, and resilience. Individuals can reach their wellness goals by recognising the root causes of cravings, employing practical management measures, and cultivating mindful eating habits. The idea is to approach urges with knowledge and compassion, making mindful decisions that support your overall health and well-being.

Chapter 10:
Promoting Mindful Living for Long-Term Wellness

Long-term wellness is about building lasting habits and practices that support general well-being over time, rather than relying on fast solutions. We will look at how to improve mindful living to promote long-term wellness, including practical tactics and ideas that may be applied to everyday life.

The Importance Of Mindful Living

Mindful living is about embracing life with intention, mindfulness, and compassion. Individuals who practise mindfulness in various aspects of their lives can build resilience, reduce stress, and feel more satisfied and fulfilled.

Key Features of Mindful Living:

1. Present Moment Awareness: Being totally involved and present in each moment, without thinking about the past or worrying about the future.

2. Nonjudgmental Acceptance: Taking things as they are, without judgment or criticism, and responding with kindness and compassion.

3. Intentional Action: Acting with purpose and intention, making decisions that are consistent with your values and priorities.

4. Self-Compassion: Being compassionate and understanding to oneself, especially during difficult or challenging circumstances.

Principles of Long-Term Wellness

To maintain long-term wellness, it is critical to follow ideas and behaviours that enhance overall health and well-being. These principles outline a framework for living thoughtfully and developing a healthy and meaningful existence.

1. Prioritize Self-Care: Set aside time and energy to engage in activities that nourish your body, mind, and spirit.

2. Cultivate Resilience: Increase your resilience by learning coping skills, cultivating a positive mindset, and learning from trials and disappointments.

3. Nurture Relationships: Make meaningful connections with others by encouraging open communication, empathy, and mutual support.

4. Embrace Balance: Aim for balance in all aspects of life, such as work, relationships, leisure, and self-care. Avoid extremes and instead prioritise moderation.

Effective Strategies for Long-Term Wellness

Improving mindful living for long-term wellness entails establishing practical tactics and routines that promote general health and well-being. Here are some strategies to consider

.

1. Practice Gratitude: Begin a daily gratitude practice by thinking about what you are grateful for. This can promote a good attitude and boost emotions of happiness and well-being.

2. Set Boundaries: To avoid burnout and overwhelm, set clear boundaries for your time, energy, and responsibilities. Learn to say no to activities or obligations that do not match your priorities.

3. Exercise Regularly: Incorporate regular physical activity into your routine to improve physical health, reduce stress, and improve mood. Find activities that you enjoy and incorporate them into your regular agenda.

4. Prioritize Sleep: Make sleep a top priority by developing a soothing bedtime ritual, avoiding caffeine and devices before bed, and aiming for 7-9 hours of quality sleep per night.

5. Mindful Technology Use: Set limitations on screen time, take breaks away from devices, and be deliberate about how you use technology to enhance your well-being.

6. Nourish Your Body: Eat full, nutritious foods that promote total health and vitality. Pay attention to hunger and fullness cues, and engage in mindful eating.

7. **Manage Stress**: Learn stress-reduction strategies like deep breathing, meditation, yoga, or journaling to lessen the impact of stress on your physical and mental health.

Developing Mindful Habits for Long-term Wellness

Cultivating mindful behaviours is critical for ensuring long-term wellness and maintaining good lifestyle choices. Here are a few habits to develop:

1. Morning Routine: Begin each day with a mindful morning routine that includes activities like meditation, writing, or stretching to create a good tone for the day.

2. Mindful Movement: Include mindful movement techniques like yoga, tai chi, or walking meditation in your daily routine to improve your physical and mental health.

3. Regular Check-Ins: Take regular breaks during the day to check in with yourself and examine your physical, emotional, and mental well-being. Adjust your activities or routines as needed to maintain your well-being.

4. Mindful Eating: Practice mindful eating by paying attention to your hunger and fullness cues, savoring each bite, and remaining present during the eating experience.

Quotes to Promote Long-Term Wellness

Drawing inspiration from the wisdom of others can serve as motivation and guidance on the path to long-term wellness. Here are some quotes to think about:

1. **Lao Tzu**: *"The journey of a thousand miles begins with one step."*

2. **Dalai Lama**: *"Happiness does not come ready-made. "It stems from your own actions."*

3. **Brenda Brown:** *"Owning our story and loving ourselves through that process is the bravest thing that we'll ever do."*

4. **Ralph Waldo Emerson** *said, "The first wealth is health."*

Improving mindful living for long-term wellness entails embracing concepts and activities that promote general health and well-being. Individuals can encourage long-term success by prioritising self-care, developing resilience, nourishing connections, and embracing balance.

Chapter 11:

Strategies for Sustainable Habits and Lifestyle Changes.

Developing durable habits and lifestyle modifications is critical for long-term success in meeting health and wellness objectives. In this chapter, we will look at strategies for long-term transformation, with a focus on developing habits that are both effective and sustainable.

The Importance of Sustainability

Sustainability is essential for maintaining progress and avoiding relapse while making lifestyle changes. Instead of relying just on willpower, sustainable habits become ingrained in everyday routines, making them simpler to maintain in the long term.

Key Features of Sustainable Habits:

1. Consistency: Consistently exercising new behaviors over time strengthens habits and leads to long-term transformation.

2. Flexibility: Sustainable habits adapt to changing situations and environments, allowing for adjustments as needed.

3. Gradual Progression: Making tiny, incremental adjustments over time is more sustainable than attempting to completely revamp habits at once.

4. Self-Reflection: Regular self-reflection and adjustment enable people to stay on track and find opportunities for growth.

Strategies for Sustainable Habits Building

Lasting habits necessitates a deliberate strategy that tackles both the behavior and the circumstances that drive it. Here are some ways for building long-lasting habits:

1.Clearly identify your goals and reduce them down into smaller, more doable tasks. Concentrate on actions that are reasonable and doable given your existing situation.

2. Create a Supportive Environment: Surround yourself with people, tools, and settings that help you achieve your goals. This could include finding social support, organizing your physical area, or removing barriers to achievement.

3. Apply Implementation Intentions: Create precise action plans for how and when you will participate in new behaviors. This raises the possibility of follow-through and minimizes the need for willpower.

4. Practice Self-Compassion: Be nice to yourself when you experience setbacks, acknowledging that they are a normal part of the transition process. Approach difficulties with curiosity and a desire to learn from experience.

5. Appreciate Progress: Recognise and appreciate your accomplishments along the way, no matter how minor. Celebrating achievements increases motivation and reinforces beneficial habits.

Overcoming Common Challenges

Building sustainable habits is possible, but it is not without hurdles. Here are some frequent problems and ways to overcome them:

1. Lack of Motivation: Discover how to boost motivation by connecting with your core beliefs and reasons for making changes. Visualize the benefits of attaining your goals and remind yourself of them frequently.

2. Time Constraints: Prioritize and schedule new behaviors into your daily routine. Look for ways to blend new behaviors with old processes to increase efficiency.

3. Social Pressure: Handle social pressure by articulating your objectives to others and soliciting their help. Surround yourself with individuals who share your beliefs and aspirations, and don't be hesitant to set limits when needed.

4. Perfectionism: Give up the need to be perfect and accept imperfection as a normal part of the learning process. Focus on progress rather than perfection, and be kind with yourself when you have setbacks.

Developing Healthy Habits for Life

A particular healthy behaviors in your everyday routine can improve your long-term health and well-being. Here are some crucial behaviors you should consider incorporating into your lifestyle.

1. Regular activity: Aim for at least 150 minutes of moderate-intensity activity per week, with a combination of cardiovascular, strength, and flexibility training.

2. Eat a balanced diet rich in fruits, vegetables, whole grains, lean proteins, and healthy fats.

Practice mindful eating and pay attention to your body's hunger and fullness cues.

3. Adequate Sleep: Make sleep a priority by developing a consistent bedtime routine, creating a sleep-friendly atmosphere, and striving for 7-9 hours of quality sleep per night.

4. Stress Management: Learn effective stress management strategies like deep breathing, meditation, yoga, or relaxation exercises to lessen the negative effects of stress on your health.

5. Hydration: To stay hydrated, drink plenty of water throughout the day. Aim for at least 8 glasses of water every day, accounting for circumstances such as activity level and weather.

Quotes to Inspire Sustainable

Change Drawing inspiration from the expertise of others can provide motivation and encouragement as you work to develop long-term habits. Here are some quotes to think about:

1. James Clear: "*You do not achieve the level of your ambitions. "You fall to the level of your systems."*

2. Leo Babauta: "*Do not wait; time will never be 'just right.'" Start where you are and work with whatever tools you have at your disposal; greater tools will be discovered as you progress.*"

3. **Gretchen Rubin**: "*What you do every day matters more than what you do once in a while.*"

4. Aristotle said, "*We are what we repeatedly do." Excellence, then, is a habit rather than an act.*

Sustainable habits and lifestyle modifications are critical for long-term health and well-being. Individuals can develop habits that will help them achieve their goals for years to come by using tactics that prioritise consistency, adaptability, and self-compassion.

Conclusion:

Embracing Mindful Living for Long-Term Wellness
In our exploration of mindful eating and living, we've dived into the depths of awareness, knowledge, and application. From grasping the fundamentals of mindful eating to incorporating mindfulness into daily life, each chapter has been a step towards a more balanced and fulfilled life.

Reflecting on The Journey

As we wrap up this exploration, it's important to reflect on the journey we've taken. Mindful living is more than just a discipline; it is a way of life, approached with openness, curiosity, and compassion. It is about being totally present in each moment, accepting both the joys and hardships that life brings.

We've learned great ideas and practical ways for cultivating mindfulness in a variety of situations. Here are some crucial points to carry with you on your journey:

1. Presence: Practice being present in every moment, embracing the richness of life as it unfolds.

2. Awareness: Increase your awareness of your thoughts, feelings, and behaviors, resulting in a better understanding of yourself and your surroundings.

3. Compassion: Practice self-compassion and compassion for others, acknowledging our common humanity and interdependence.

4. Intention: Live with intention, making decisions that reflect your values and goals.

5. Resilience: Develop resilience in the face of obstacles, finding strength and wisdom in adversity.

The Power of Mindfulness

Mindfulness is more than a transitory fad or trend; it is a timeless discipline with the potential to alter people's lives. Even in the middle of modern life's hustle and chaos, incorporating mindfulness into our daily lives can provide us with greater serenity, joy, and fulfillment.

As you continue on your mindful living path, keep in mind that the goal is progress, not perfection. Every moment presents an opportunity to start over, correct direction, and align with your finest intentions. Stay open to the possibilities that each day presents, and believe in the wisdom of your own inner direction.

Finally, I encourage you to adopt mindful living as a lifelong practice, a voyage of self-discovery, growth, and transformation. May each moment be an opportunity to experience the fullness of life, and may mindfulness lead you to more peace, pleasure, and well-being. Thank you for going on this adventure with me. May your road be full with light, love, and limitless possibilities.

www.ingramcontent.com/pod-product-compliance
Lightning Source LLC
Chambersburg PA
CBHW050113230526
45470CB00004B/1811